Closed For Repairs with Plumbing Problems

David G Scott

Published by David G Scott, 2022.

While every precaution has been taken in the preparation of this book, the publisher assumes no responsibility for errors or omissions, or for damages resulting from the use of the information contained herein.

CLOSED FOR REPAIRS WITH PLUMBING PROBLEMS

First edition. February 15, 2022.

ISBN: 979-8201907204

Written by David G Scott.

Table of Contents

Chapter 1 – One Liners 1

Chapter 2 – Random Thoughts...22

Chapter 3 - Short Screenplays | Dewey Street 30

Bear With Me 38

Holy Smokes 42

Leaves 47

The Candidate 52

Medium Coffee The Medium 57

Me and Yuh 66

Baseball and Shakespeare 81

A New TV Show...97

Chapter 4 - Standup Comedy | Driving Around 106

My First Wife Sally 109

Maine... 114

John Deer.. 116

Emoji Rap 117

I'm Old... 119

Dedicated to my wife Sally, who laughed at my jokes until she couldn't.

Chapter 1 – One Liners

If you ask for change at the Dollar Store, they just give you a different dollar.

—+—

Apparently, it's inappropriate to take a couch that's sitting by the curb... if it's in front of a furniture store. I know that now.

—+—

If you laid an adult male Blue Whale lengthwise on a football field, with its nose on one goal line, you'd have to re-schedule the game.

—+—

In nursing homes, the code word for toilet is "mustard." Specifically, Grey Poupon.

—+—

Taking It To The Streets by the Doobie Brothers is my favorite song about trash day.

—+—

You know what makes me smile? Facial muscles.

—+—

I went to a catfish restaurant recently, but I was catfished - they only served trout.

—+—

I wish I'd named my son "Harley," because then he could introduce himself as Harley, David's son.

—+—

Have you noticed that Papa John has never been seen in public with his son Jimmy?

—+—

I think the Miss Universe contest should be limited to contestants who have already won a Miss Galaxy contest.

—+—

That sound you hear when you close the cupboard and hear something fall? That's the sound of someone else's problem.

—+—

At the store, a dad bought his kid some candy and said, "Don't tell Mom," and winked at me, so now I'm caught up in their web of lies.

—+—

I don't have any tattoos, but if I ever get one, it will be a tattoo of more muscles.

—+—

I love the time of night when I'm alone in the house, everything's quiet and I can walk around wearing nothing by my knee brace.

—+—

What exactly is a cold-blooded killer? Someone who murders reptiles?

—+—

In Spanish, Sponge Bob Square Pants is Sponge Roberto Square Pantalones.

—+—

Apartments aren't apart; they're together. They should be called "togetherments."

—+—

Shout out to my four favorite bags: barf, grab, punching and Poppa's Got a Brand New.

—+—

If I've said it once, I've said it 1,000 times – I can't keep track of how many times I've said something.

—+—

Whoever said "Words can't hurt me" has never been hit with a dictionary.

—+—

"Hermit crab" describes me twice.

—+—

I give 110% about 30% of the time.

—+—

In a duel, my weapon of choice would be a t-shirt cannon.

—+—

Christian rock is the only music that's performed in both heaven and hell.

—+—

Apparently, it's inappropriate to RSVP to a wedding invitation by saying, "I can't make it. Sorry. Maybe next time."

—+—

This morning, I found a spider in my sock drawer, which was very disturbing because it belongs in the spider drawer.

—+—

I named my phone "Elvis" because it dies every time I'm on the toilet.

—+—

When God closes a door, he doesn't open a window because God's not air conditioning the whole neighborhood.

—+—

The hardest part of owning a pet is taking personal responsibility for rain.

—+—

I like coffee, but if I drink too much I realize there are tiny spiders under my scalp, weaving hair.

—+—

Let us take a moment to be grateful our internal organs don't itch.

—+—

I like ground pepper, so now I'm looking for air pepper and sea pepper, because I want to support all three branches of the pepper military.

—+—

If a hysterectomy is hers, and a hernia is his, shouldn't they be called a "hisnia" and a "hersterectomy"?

—+—

Exactly how dead is a doornail?

—+—

When I go hiking, I take a big bottle that's a combination of water to stay hydrated, a sports drink to keep my electrolytes balanced, and cappuccino because HIKING! WHO WANT TO GO HIKING? C'MON! LET'S HIKE!

—+—

My two favorite kinds of songs are songs about love and songs that welcome me to the jungle.

—+—

Recently, I ate an entire can of Pringles. I was very disappointed because there were only three of them, and they were tennis ball flavored.

—+—

If you own a nice pair of shoes, you don't need to spend money on dog toys.

—+—

My cousin is starting a small piano store; next week is the baby grand opening.

—+—

If you're smoking a cigarette while riding a bike, there's a 98% chance you're headed to the liquor store.

—+—

One good thing about having the stomach flu is rediscovering your love of Ginger Ale.

—+—

If you hear weird noises in the night, make weirder noises to establish dominance.

—+—

I wish tire companies would put confetti in their tires, because if you have a blowout, it would still be kind of an okay day.

—+—

Keep an eye out for my new cookbook entitled "It's Expired – Throw It Away."

—+—

I want to be in one of those Chevy commercials, wait for them to reveal the cars, then freak out so violently I would have to be tranquilized.

—+—

Note to self: When you're putting chocolate powder on your coffee, if you say "Get wild. Get crazy. You earned it." out loud, others can hear you.

—+—

Rather than kill that spider, I started telling it about my fantasy football team and it left peacefully on its own.

—+—

Speaking of fantasy football, how can it be "fantasy" if there are no unicorns?

—+—

I can't say for sure, but I think the job I just did emptying the dishwasher will be the one I'm remembered for.

—+—

Yesterday, I saved the life of a trash bag by slamming on my brakes.

—+—

I've started saying I'm allergic to foods I don't like; it's just easier.

—+—

Darth Vader could fall asleep in Imperial meetings and nobody would notice.

—+—

Beauty and the Beast is a triumph, reminding little girls that even if your boyfriend is a monster with rage issues, you can change him.

—+—

The first guy to hear a parrot talk was probably not okay for a few days.

—+—

I just accidentally hit my elbow on the table and it hurt so bad that I unintentionally summoned the ghosts of my ancestors.

—+—

Any shoes are running shoes if you're running.

—+—

I love waking up to the sound of birds arguing with their spouses.

—+—

Never mind. Here's your money back. I'm really sorry.

- Me, as a Life Coach

—+—

It's amazing how much better you feel after a hot shower and a frontal lobotomy.

—+—

The Friday the 13th movies would be a lot better if every once in a while they cut to a hockey team saying "Hey! Where's our goalie?!"

—+—

Today I helped an elderly man cross the street by repeatedly honking my horn.

—+—

Once you realize that there is no right way to load a dishwasher you can finally live free.

—+—

You should be able to twist the bottom of the Pringles can to bring the chips to the top like a Chapstick.

—+—

My next pet is going to be named "Peeves" and I will introduce it as my pet Peeves, and it would never stop being funny to me.

—+—

Did we ever figure out what the knights in white sat in?

—+—

I want to set up one of those "escape rooms" where the clues are all meaningless and there is no solution... oh wait... that's life.

—+—

Whoever decided to use full volume doorbell noises in their commercials has never owned a dog.

—+—

The people who think I'm extremely lazy are going to feel real stupid when they find out I made my bed this morning.

—+—

The voice in my head is an exceptionally good singer.

—+—

I believe that Friday the 13th is a holiday started by Big Hockey to sell more masks.

—+—

My action figure is me lying on the couch watching Netflix, but you have to buy the little TV separately.

—+—

When I was at the mall, I saw a child being pushed around in a stroller and being offered snacks to stop crying. I wanted to ask him how he got that job.

—+—

You guys, I just ate a salad... that wasn't inside a cheeseburger!

—+—

If you're feeling stressed, just relax, take a deep breath, and then exhale fire over all of your enemies. (Actually, this is more for dragons.)

—+—

I'm going to start an "Earth, Wind & Fire" tribute band called "Dirt, Breeze & Heat."

—+—

In Jurassic Park, if you replace the velociraptors with geese, it would be equally entertaining and terrifying.

—+—

Fred Flintstone was the first man to become a vitamin.

—+—

I enjoy any movie where someone tries to blow a trumpet, it doesn't work, then they shake it and an animal falls out.

—+—

Dogs probably destroy shoes because they see humans put them on before they leave.

—+—

I bet Dr. Frankenstein didn't know what to call his monster, so he just said "Hey, dude" a lot.

—+—

Just watched a video about a snake that learned how to open doors, which is great because sleeping and feeling safe are highly overrated.

—+—

One day I'll look back on my life and realize all the really great days were the ones when I had a grilled cheese sandwich.

—+—

If aliens actually attack Earth, my first thought will probably be "Which movie came the closest?"

—+—

I'm a liberal, but mostly in regard to the amount of cream cheese I spread on a bagel.

—+—

I'm not sure why every fast food restaurant commercial doesn't show wild animals devouring their food like there's no tomorrow.

—+—

Do they sell calendars by the month? I'm not sure I want to commit to a full year.

—+—

Live every day like you're being taped by one of those shows that sees if you'd help the person who just fell down in front of you.

—+—

Every year during the Macy's Thanksgiving Day Parade there's at least one person who stops, looks around, and says "Guys, what the heck are we doing with our lives?"

—+—

When one door closes, push a dresser in front of it and jump out the window.

—+—

Imagine how rough your life in prison would be if you got busted by a crime solving dog.

—+—

If you're not starting balloon fights using balloons filled with creamed corn instead of water, you need to level up.

—+—

One thing I really enjoy about the NBA Finals is that regardless of a game's outcome, several millionaires will have their night ruined.

—+—

I want to be rich enough to buy a Jeep and replace the spare tire on the back with a giant glazed donut.

—+—

"You can't bark like that and expect to get anywhere in life" – something I once said to a dog.

—+—

I'm jealous of armadillos; they can curl into a ball and lie there and everyone thinks it's normal.

—+—

Sometimes I yawn so hard I look like a snake trying to eat large prey.

—+—

Sometimes, when I can't sleep, I just lay there, thinking about how someone in America has an ancestor who was the first person ever to get hit by a car.

—+—

I dropped my phone down the stairs but luckily it didn't break because it was in my pocket.

—+—

I don't want to get too political on here but I definitely believe in the death penalty for my alarm clock.

—+—

Million dollar idea: a smoke alarm that turns off when you yell "I'm just cooking!"

—+—

No matter our skin, our gender, our culture or our family, we all have one thing in common - none of us floss regularly.

—+—

Some mornings it's hard to make the coffee when you haven't had any coffee.

—+—

They say it's healthy for your lawn to change the way you mow it, so next time I mow I'm going to do it in heels.

—+—

I'd be a lot more into politics if instead of politics they were tacos.

—+—

The best thing about getting older is crawling into bed after a long day to hear your joints make the sound of a semi releasing its air brakes.

—+—

If you ever see me spacing off, I'm most likely reliving that touchdown I scored during recess in 5th grade.

—+—

Every time a comedian dies, and somebody says "They're making God laugh now." I say, "Can't God just watch Airplane?"

—+—

Caterpillars have the ideal life; they eat a lot and then sleep for a while and wake up absolutely beautiful.

—+—

I judge people by the number of things I have to move off the passenger seat when I get in their car.

—+—

I just started my new job and I've already replied to all the emails from my boss with "unsubscribe".

—+—

I'm going to open a restaurant with giant portions called "The Unbuttoned Jeans".

—+—

Exercise? I thought you said "extra fries". □

—+—

I miss the days before gluten when all we had to worry about was total nuclear annihilation.

—+—

I just walked into a spider web and my reaction could have won a 1938 Jitterbug contest.

—+—

Even on my regular antidepressant, I still felt unresolved symptoms of depression. So I asked my doctor about adding chips and salsa.

—+—

Let's fix the obesity problem and improve hand-eye coordination by replacing vending machines with claw machines and make people earn their snacks.

—+—

I hate when I try to take a really cute selfie and it gets photobombed by my age. ☐[1]

—+—

I wish electronic devices would scream a little bit when you unplugged them.

—+—

I just found out I'm pregnant. At least that's what the expectant mother sign says for my parking spot.

—+—

My phone just filmed a three-hour documentary about my life inside my pocket.

—+—

Instead of going to Starbucks, I make my own coffee, yell my name out, and light a $5 bill on fire.

—+—

Turns out the best way to be successful is to work hard and be talented, which is very annoying.

—+—

---

1. https://www.facebook.com/hashtag/usa?source=feed_text&story_id=10153033055528484

While at the convenience store I saw a teenage girl standing by herself
and not on her phone – I hope she's okay.

—+—

I'm going to be so pissed if when we finally get to ask the aliens about
crop circles they say, "We just really hate corn."

—+—

I can't decide if people who wear pajamas in public have given up on
life or are living life to the fullest.

—+—

I had this great idea in the shower this morning: go back to sleep.

—+—

The adult life I imagined as a child involved less laundry and more
group singing and dance numbers.

—+—

This oatmeal tastes like I'm going to need a couple donuts.

—+—

I'm on a new diet called "I have $10 till next Friday."

—+—

Apparently, when people say "I could use a hand" it doesn't mean they
want to get slapped in the face.

—+—

A large bug just fell onto my shoulder and disappeared, so if anyone needs me I'll be walking around my house with a flamethrower.

—+—

The problem with taking the road less traveled is poor cell phone service.

—+—

I haven't always been fat. I once weighed 8lbs 9oz.

—+—

Hard work never killed anyone, but why risk it?

—+—

Fun fact: In 1965, the acoustic eel became the electric eel causing outrage among its fans.

—+—

Sometimes I consider myself a badass then I realize the most dangerous thing I might do today is sneeze while driving.

—+—

There are a lot of songs about partying, but not a lot about how it's going to be a big day tomorrow so we should really get to bed early guys.

—+—

I was going to go out and have drinks with friends tonight, but my bank account told me I'm staying home and watching cat videos on YouTube.

—+—

I always keep at least six wigs in my car for trips to the grocery store so I can keep going back for free samples.

—+—

Sometimes, for good luck, I like to throw spare change into the chocolate fountain at Golden Corral.

—+—

My stomach just made a noise like a really old door opening.

—+—

Sometimes at my job I shout "GREAT WORK THIS WEEK EVERYBODY!" into every bathroom I walk past.

—+—

I'm only a little bit hungry. I could only eat a pony.

—+—

Whoever said "We have nothing to fear but fear itself" obviously never accidentally hit Reply All.

—+—

You can catch more flies with a long sticky projectile tongue than with vinegar.

—+—

Tomorrow, I am giving a new meaning to the phrase "sleeping around" by taking naps in a bunch of different places.

—+—

At this point why don't they just open a charter school for kids that don't have a peanut allergy?

—+—

If they made cockroach-print tiles, my kitchen décor would be all set.

—+—

Sometimes I wonder what Water did to get kicked out of Earth, Wind & Fire.

—+—

I feel like people don't even consider my schedule when they get into car wrecks.

—+—

I'm old enough to remember car accidents before texting.

—+—

Does running late count as exercise?

—+—

A hat and a cape used to mean you were well-off; now it means you're in a marching band.

—+—

If I had one word to describe myself it would be "bad at following directions."

—+—

If life gives you melons, you might be dyslexic.

—+—

I am one of a kind. I'm not sure which kind, but I do know I am one of them.

—+—

I wonder why some people feel that using their turn signal will somehow reveal their plans to the enemy.

—+—

I just read '100 Things To Do Before You Die,' and I'm really surprised 'Yell for help' wasn't one of them.

—+—

I've been doing some soul-searching and all I've found is a gum wrapper and an old sock. That can't be good.

—+—

Saying something over and over again doesn't make it true—unless you're saying, "I'm obnoxious and repetitive."

—+—

I used to have a dog that I named Miss Wendy. I wish I'd named her Karma, so I could truthfully say, "Karma is a bitch."

Chapter 2 – Random Thoughts

———

MY COUSIN IS A KLEPTOMANIAC – he keeps picking things up. His brother is a manokleptiac – he keeps putting things back. They can't go grocery shopping together.

—+—

Pablo Picasso's full name was "Pablo Diego José Francisco de Paula Juan Nepomuceno María de los Remedios Cipriano de la Santísima Trinidad Ruiz y Picasso." Imagine his poor teacher the first day of school with a roomful of Picasso's. She took roll, then it was time for lunch.

—+—

Invisible to the naked eye. As opposed to what? A semi-naked eye? An eye wearing a lovely spring outfit?

—+—

A friend posted on Facebook that she bought a weighted blanked. I posted that at my age, every blanket is a weighted blanket.

—+—

A friend posted on Facebook "I hope you know you're capable, brave and significant. Even when it feels like you're not." Curiously, that's exactly what I say every morning to my digestive system.

—+—

A friend posted on Facebook that she was looking for a plumber to replace her water heater. I posted it would be better to replace her water heater with another water heater.

—+—

Don: I'm really tired. Sunglasses tired.

Me: Sunglasses tired? What's that?

Don: I'm too tired to get my sunglasses so I can put them on.

Me: Where are they?

Don: In my pocket.

—+—

A friend posted on Facebook that she'd found some cinnamon rolls to die for. I posted that if she ate enough of them, they'd be to die from.

—+—

Subway Sandwich Shop has a Black Forest Ham sandwich. What is that, exactly? Is that pink ham from the black forest? Or is it black ham from the green forest? I think to avoid confusion they should rename it Pink Green Black Forest Ham.

—+—

What is a Japanese tea garden? Is it a garden where Japanese people drink tea, or a garden where everyone drinks Japanese tea? I know it's not both, because that would be a Japanese Japanese tea garden.

—+—

What is wild bird seed? Is it wild seed for tame birds? That would be called "wild tame bird seed." Is it tame seed for wild birds? That would be called "tame wild bird seed." Is it wild seed for wild birds? That would be called "wild wild bird seed." One thing I know for sure – it's not tame seed for tame birds, because that's called "parakeet food."

Sometimes I confuse "window shopping" and "shop lifting." The other day I was at a store in the mall, and the store manager asked if he could help me find something. I thought I told him I was just window shopping. A few minutes later I was having a very uncomfortable conversation with mall security. After I explained how I get confused, we laughed, and then he suggested I continue shopping... at a different mall... for the rest of my life.

I dated a girl who wasn't voted "Miss Kansas City" or "Miss Platte County." She was voted "Miss Cellanious," probably because her favorite phrase was "Whatever."

When I was a teenager I was in a gang. We called ourselves The Electrical Workers Union Local 412. Our gang color was bright orange, which we wore on reflective vests. We wore hard hats backwards because we were rebels. Our gang symbol was the same symbol utility companies use to indicate where to install a streetlight. Let me tell you, our neighborhood was very well lit.

The Missouri legislature is considering a law to make it legal to break a car window to rescue a pet. I'm in favor of it because the last time I broke a car window to rescue a purse, I got arrested!

—+—

My cousin's an ornithologist. His specialty is the Hoot Owl, but he's discovered some other rare owls. He discovered the Cute Owl. Instead of going "Hoo... hoo...," it goes "Awww... awww." He also discovered the Toot Owl. Instead of going "Hoo..." it goes "Pfffat." And that is my only fart joke. Thank you.

—+—

My cousin is an agnostic. An agnostic is someone who wakes up every morning and wonders whether or not there's a God. I'm more of an eggnostic. I wake up every morning wondering whether or not to have an omelet.

—+—

My cousin's band has trouble getting gigs. I blame the name they've chosen for the band, which is Closed For Repairs. And when they get a gig, they have trouble getting people to come hear them play. I blame the fact they always perform with their favorite band, Plumbing Problems. Because the marquee reads, "Tonight Only! Closed For Repairs with Plumbing Problems!"

—+—

Shoehorn is a funny word, like it's a musical instrument.

Announcer: Ladies and gentlemen, please welcome tonight's special guest Herr Hermann Erhardt, virtuoso on the shoehorn. He'll be playing his own composition, Toccata and Fugue in 10½ Wide for Flugelhorn, Coronet and Reeboks.

—+—

Dyslectics have a tough time living in our world because their brains reverse things. My cousin is dyslectic. He likes Wisconsin barbeque and Kansas City cheese. He likes French whiskey and Irish wine. He likes corn from Vermont and maple syrup from Nebraska. Fortunately, his name is Bob.

If I owned a race car, I'd name it Palindrome. Because then I could say, "Palindrome is a race car. Race car is a palindrome." Because it would be the same forwards and backwards.

They say the road to hell is paved with good intentions. They say the streets in heaven are paved with gold. I say we have seriously underestimated the strength of the Pavers Union.

My cousin is allergic to pollen... and Kleenex. In the spring, his eyes water, so he grabs a Kleenex, then starts to sneeze. I suggested he switch to Baby Wipes, because nobody's allergic to babies.

Whenever the teller at a fast food restaurant asks for my name, I say "Alex Underwood, but use my initials, A.U." When they call out "A.U." I yell back, "'Hey, you?' Is that any way to talk to a customer?"

Me: Just because I imagine having conversations with inanimate objects that doesn't mean I'm crazy.

My coffee: If you say so.

—+—

I gave a clerk a $50 bill, and she got out a counterfeit pen. I said,

"How do you know the pen's not counterfeit?"

"What?"

"What you need is a pen to tell if the counterfeit pen is counterfeit."

"What are you talking about?"

"You need a *counterfeit* counterfeit pen *pen*."

She didn't say anything, so I kept going.

"Then you would need a pen to see if the counterfeit counterfeit pen pen were counterfeit."

She still didn't say anything, so I kept going.

"You know, a *counterfeit* counterfeit counterfeit pen pen *pen*."

She finally looked at me and said, "Here's your change, Sparky, now get out!"

Which was very disturbing because my name's not Sparky.

—+—

Hiring manager: So, how would you describe yourself?

Me: Terse.

—+—

Sun: *goes down*

Animals: Goodnight.

Crickets: Who wants to PARTY?

—+—

My yoga instructor sets the bar very low. She said,

"If you're practicing mindful breathing, you're practicing yoga."

"What do you mean?"

"Do this. Breathe in through your nose... and out through your mouth. In through your nose... out through your mouth."

"That's very relaxing."

"Good! That will be $20."

—+—

Me: I'm an expert at identifying birds.

Coworker: Okay, what about those ones flying over that building?

Me: Yup, those are birds.

—+—

Me: I'm gonna take a shower.

Spider in my bathtub: Nope.

—+—

Hiring manager: So, tell me just a little about you. What are you doing currently?

Me: I'm applying for a job.

—+—

My cousin recently lost his faith. He's what the church calls an "apostate" – someone who has fallen away. Recently, he was at the doctor's office for a prostate exam. The doctor, instead of asking him to bend over, asked him to lie down on the table. My cousin asked,

"Why?"

"Because I've never given a prostate exam to an apostate who was prostrate."

"What?"

"Because I've never given a prostate exam to a prostrate apostate."

"You mean the old prostrate apostate prostate exam? Why didn't you say so?"

Chapter 3 - Short Screenplays
Dewey Street

———

FADE IN.

1 INT – LIVING ROOM

A doorbell rings. Jerad walks to the front door and opens it.

JERAD

Cousin Bryce! It's good to see you! How have you been?

BRYCE

Good! I was driving around doing some errands, and I thought I'd drop by.

JERAD

Great! Hey, I'm just heading out to catch a movie. Want to come along?

BRYCE

Absolutely! I'll drive.

JERAD

Oh, don't bother. It's just a short walk from here.

BRYCE

It's what?

JERAD

A short walk.

BRYCE

What's a Shore Twalk?

JERAD

What?

BRYCE

I'm familiar with the Mountain Twalk and the Prairie Twalk. In fact, I think I saw a Prairie Twalk one time outside Omaha. Beautiful plumage.

JERAD

What are you talking about?

BRYCE

The Shore Twalk.

JERAD

Yes, that's what it is. Anyway, to get there all we do is go out the front door and walk up Dewey Street.

BRYCE

We walk up what?

JERAD

Dewey Street.

BRYCE

Do we street? I don't know. How do you "street"?

JERAD

What?

BRYCE

You said we go out the front door and walk up. Do we street?

JERAD

That's right.

BRYCE

I don't know.

JERAD

You don't know?

BRYCE

I don't know how to "street."

JERAD

No, not Howto Street, Dewey street.

BRYCE

I don't know.

JERAD

Why not? I just told you.

BRYCE

(Irritated.) No, you didn't! Here's an idea: let's watch Netflix.

JERAD

Calm down! Listen, the theater is right around the corner. When we get to the corner, we turn left.

BRYCE

Right.

JERAD

No, if you turn right, you'll be left behind.

BRYCE

What?

JERAD

If you turn right, you'll be left.

BRYCE

So I turn left?

JERAD

Right.

BRYCE

So I turn right?

JERAD

No, if you turn right, you'll be wrong.

BRYCE

Do I turn left?

JERAD

Right!

BRYCE

(Angry) Make up your mind!

JERAD

Tap the brakes. Calm down. Let's move past the corner.

BRYCE

At this point, I'm not sure I want to go anywhere...

JERAD

Take a deep breath. We're almost to the theater.

BRYCE

Finally! What's the name of the theater?

JERAD

It's called The We Don't Walk Theater.

BRYCE

The what theater?

JERAD

We Don't Walk.

BRYCE

We don't walk?

JERAD

Yes.

BRYCE

Good. I'll drive.

JERAD

No, it's just a short walk.

BRYCE

(Angry) Don't start over!!!

JERAD

What are you talking about? I told you we're at the theater.

BRYCE

We don't walk?

JERAD

That's right.

BRYCE

Then how are we going to get there?

JERAD

We walk.

BRYCE

(Angry) How about I put punch you in the mouth?

JERAD

No, no, no. Relax! Take a deep breath. I told you everything we need to do. Just repeat it back to me. You'll see.

BRYCE

This is not going to work.

JERAD

Yes, it will. Just tell me how to get to the theater.

BRYCE

Ok. Here we go. (He takes a deep breath.) We started out talking about a bird, the Shore Twalk. Why, I'll never know. Anyway, to get to the theater we go out the front door and walk up. Do we street? I don't know. I don't know how to "street." When we get to the corner, we take a right to be left and left to be right and a right to be wrong. At this point I don't know what I'm doing, but we do walk to the theater we don't walk. How'd I do?

JERAD

Perfect.

BRYCE

(Angry) I don't even know what I'm talking about! But I do know this: if we ever get there, I'm going to strangle you!

JERAD

What?

BRYCE

I'm going to strangle you!

JERAD

Oh, that's the name of the movie!

BRYCE

AAUUUGGGHHH!!!! (Opens the front door and leaves.)

JERAD

(Leaning out the door) Ok, maybe we could watch TV?

Fade out.

Bear With Me

—

FADE IN.

1 COMPUTER SCREEN

Two men are in a Zoom meeting.

                    MIKE

          Today has been crazy. Sorry for running late.

                    DAVID

          No problem.

                    MIKE

          So bear with me.

                    DAVID

          What?

                    MIKE

          Bear with me.

                    DAVID

          You have a bear with you?

                    MIKE

          What?

                    DAVID

I hope it's a Teddy bear, not a real bear, because that would be very dangerous.

MIKE

What are you talking about?

DAVID

You said, "Bear. With. Me."

MIKE

No, no, no. You don't get it. Bear with me means "Be patient with me."

DAVID

Ok...?

MIKE

You know, the word "bear" has other meanings, like "Bear right."

DAVID

There's a bear on your right?

MIKE

No, bear right means turn right.

DAVID

Like the fork in the road?

MIKE

Yes, like Yogi Berra said, "When you come to a fork in the road, take it."

DAVID

Yogi Bear? The one who lives in Jellystone Park?

MIKE

No, not Yogi Bear, Yogi Berra. No relation.

DAVID

Good, because I'm not a fan of bears.

MIKE

What about the right to bear arms?

DAVID

You have bear arms? Big, hairy arms with giant claws?

MIKE

No.

DAVID

Ok, good. So, you have small, teddy bear arms with cute little paws?

MIKE

Again, no. It's the second amendment. The right to bear arms.

DAVID

Bare arms? The right to wear sleeveless shirts?

MIKE

No, not bare arms, the right to have weapons.

DAVID

Good, because I might need a weapon… in case I see a bear.

MIKE

Listen, the point is I'm sorry I'm late.

DAVID

No problem. It turns out you caught me at a bad time. I just need a minute to finish up here, so bear with me.

MIKE

What?

Fade out.

Holy Smokes

FADE IN.

1 INT – LIVING ROOM – DAY

A door bell sounds. DANA walks to the front door and opens it. We see COUSIN PAUL standing outside.

DANA

Cousin Paul! I haven't seen you in a while. Come on in.

COUSIN PAUL walks in.

COUSIN PAUL

Thanks! I was in the neighborhood and thought I'd drop by.

DANA

I'm glad you did. So, what's new?

COUSIN PAUL

Big news! I switched cigarette brands.

DANA

That's the big news?

COUSIN PAUL

It's kind of a big deal. I smoked Marlboro for years, but I've switched to American Spirit cigarettes. I just call them "Spirits."

DANA

That's all you smoke now? Wholly Spirits?

COUSIN PAUL

What?

DANA

You know, totally. Totally Spirits. Exclusively Spirits. Wholly Spirits.
Get it? Ha!

COUSIN PAUL

I guess. But here's the deal. My wife doesn't want me to smoke at all, so
she takes a sewing needle and pokes holes in my packs of cigarettes.

DANA

So all of your cigarettes have holes in them?

COUSIN PAUL

Yeah. It's very annoying. They're tough to smoke.

DANA

So now they're hole-y Spirits.

COUSIN PAUL

What?

DANA

Spirit cigarettes with holes in them. Hole-y Spirits.

COUSIN PAUL

Hmmm.

DANA

So you smoke wholly hole-y Spirits. Get it? Ha!

COUSIN PAUL

Cute. But my wife wants me to stop smoking. She says when I light one, I go through some kind of ritual... almost like I worship them.

DANA

So she thinks Spirit cigarettes are holy?

COUSIN PAUL

What?

DANA

If you worship them, they must be holy. Holy Spirits.

COUSIN PAUL

Uh-oh.

DANA

So you smoke wholly hole-y Holy Spirits? Get it? Ha!

COUSIN PAUL

I get it. I get it. Anyway, I should be going.

DANA

Ok. Tell your wife I said hello.

COUSIN PAUL

I will, but I'm sure not going to let her run my life.

DANA

That's the spirit! In fact, that's the wholly hole-y Holy Spirits spirit!

COUSIN PAUL

No. No, it isn't.

DANA

Next time you come by, we'll drink to it!

COUSIN PAUL

Drink to what?

DANA

We'll have some whiskey to celebrate your attitude to carry on smoking the brand of cigarette you worship, even if your wife pokes holes in them.

COUSIN PAUL

What?

DANA

You know, we'll have some spirits.

COUSIN PAUL

Please stop.

DANA

We'll have some wholly hole-y Holy Spirits spirit spirits! Get it? Ha!

COUSIN PAUL

Enough! Are you off your meds? Holy smokes!

DANA

(Yells.) That's what I've been talking about!!!

COUSIN PAUL stares at Dana, then turns and walks out the front door.

DANA moves to the front door and yells.

DANA

Holy smokes! Get it! Ha!

Fade out.

Leaves

FADE IN.

INT. - LIBRARY

Chris walks up to the counter.

CHRIS

Hi! My name is Chris Brown. Did Professor Anderson leave something for me?

LIBRARIAN

Which Professor Anderson? There are several.

CHRIS

Dr. Anderson from the Biology Department.

LIBRARIAN

Lief Anderson?

CHRIS

That's right.

LIBRARIAN

We call him "Lief the Leaf."

CHRIS

Hahaha! Why? Because he teaches botany?

LIBRARIAN

Exactly! So you want to know if Lief left something for you?

CHRIS

Yes.

LIBRARIAN

What was it exactly?

CHRIS

Some leaves.

LIBRARIAN

That's not unusual. He occasionally leaves leaves.

CHRIS

What?

LIBRARIAN

Occasionally, Lief leaves leaves.

CHRIS

Sleeves?

LIBRARIAN

What?

CHRIS

You said, "Occasionally, Lief leaves sleeves."

LIBRARIAN

No, I didn't. Listen. Occasionally, Lief. Leaves. Leaves.

CHRIS

(Smiling) Yeah, that makes more sense.

LIBRARIAN

I don't think he ever leaves sleeves.

CHRIS

Exactly. I mean, why would he? So, is Dr. Anderson here?

LIBRARIAN

No, Lief left.

CHRIS

Haha! Did Lief leave leaves for me today, or did Lief leave without leaving leaves?

LIBRARIAN

Good one! I'm not sure about that, but I am sure that he left.

CHRIS

Can you check to see if he left leaves for me?

LIBRARIAN

What's your name again?

CHRIS

Chris Brown.

LIBRARIAN

Leave it to me. Ha! See what I did there? (Looks around.) No, apparently, Lief the Leaf left without leaving leaves.

CHRIS

Ha! So, today when Lief the Leaf left, there was no leaf left behind?

LIBRARIAN

Exactly!

CHRIS

Where did he go?

LIBRARIAN

I think to the hockey game. He's a big Toronto fan.

CHRIS

The Toronto Maple Leafs?

LIBRARIAN

Yes. We call the team "Lief's Leafs."

CHRIS

Hahaha! So, you're saying that sometimes Lief the Leaf leaves to watch Leaf's Leafs.

LIBRARIAN

You got it!

CHRIS

So, to summarize, sometimes Lief the Leaf leaves and leaves leaves. Sometimes, Lief the Leaf leaves to watch Lief's Leafs. Today, Lief the Leaf left and left no leaf behind.

LIBRARIAN

Hahaha! I couldn't have said it better myself.

CHRIS

Ok, thanks for your help.

LIBRARIAN

Sure.

CHRIS leaves. LIBRARIAN goes back to work and discovers a plastic bag with some leaves in it. LIBRARIAN reads the note on the bag.

LIBRARIAN

Oh, no. (Follows CHRIS) Chris! Wait! Don't leave without your leaves!

Fade out.

The Candidate

FADE IN.

1 INT – CONFERENCE ROOM

Seated at a large table are four writers and the Head Writer.

HEAD WRITER

Listen up. We just got a request some political ads from a candidate for Platte County Sheriff. Let's brainstorm some ideas for this account. Just anything that comes to mind.

WRITER 1

Ok. Give us some background info. What's he like?

HEAD WRITER

His name is Bob Warhammer, and he's an outsider, running for his first office. He's a law and order guy, retired Green Beret, and needs an ad that will clearly separate him from the pack.

WRITER 1

How about something like this? We start with a map of Platte County...

2 BLUE SCREEN

Writer 1 (Voice over)

We see a map of Platte County, which fades to an American Flag. Bob Warhammer marches in, stops, turns, comes to parade rest, and looks at the camera.

BOB WARHAMMER

I'm Bob Warhammer. I walk the streets at night. I hear dogs barking. I want to know what them dogs is barking at. Don't you?

3 INT – CONFERENCE ROOM

Silence. They all stare at Writer 1.

HEAD WRITER

That's it?

WRITER 1

Yeah. Simple, direct, military, gets the message across.

HEAD WRITER

Message? What message? Alright, alright. Just throwing ideas around. No bad ideas in a brainstorming session. Anyone else?

WRITER 2

How about something off the wall?

HEAD WRITER

Let's hear it.

4 BLUE SCREEN

WRITER 2 (Voice over)

We see a map of Platte County, which fades to an American Flag. Bob Warhammer marches in, stops, turns, comes to parade rest, and looks at the camera.

BOB WARHAMMER

I'm Bob Warhammer. I know pies. And I know how to handle them pie rustlers. I can smell 'em.

5 INT – CONFERENCE ROOM

HEAD WRITER

Pie rustlers?

WRITER 2

Yep. The old west. Tough lawman. Separates him from the other candidates, for sure.

HEAD WRITER

I'm going to separate you from this brainstorming session! C'mon, people! Get serious. Anyone else?

WRITER 3

How about something emphasizing his support of the Fifth Amendment? That always works.

HEAD WRITER

There you go! Let's hear it.

6 BLUE SCREEN

WRITER 3 (Voice over)

We see a map of Platte County, which fades to an American Flag. Bob Warhammer marches in, stops, turns, comes to parade rest, and looks at the camera.

BOB WARHAMMER

I'm Bob Warhammer. I know how to handle a gun. On weekends, I like nothin' better than shooting cans. Of corn. Off the shelves of grocery stores. From the parking lot. Lying in the bed of my pickup.

7 INT – CONFERENCE ROOM

All stare at WRITER 3.

WRITER 3

Hey! Lots of people in Platte County own a gun.

HEAD WRITER

Ok, enough horseplay. Let's focus. We've got to come up with something or we're going to lose this account.

WRITER 4

How about something else Platte County voters enjoy – fishing.

HEAD WRITER

Let's hear it.

8 BLUE SCREEN

WRITER 4 (Voice over)

We see a map of Platte County, which fades to an American Flag. Bob Warhammer marches in, stops, turns, comes to parade rest, and looks at the camera.

BOB WARHAMMER

Me and my buddy went fishing the other day. So we gathered up some M-80's, got in my pickup and drove down to the pond. We lit them M-80's and tossed 'em in the pond. No luck. Then we remembered that pond wasn't even there last year.

9 INT – CONFERENCE ROOM

HEAD WRITER

Fishing with explosives? Isn't that illegal?

WRITER 4

You're not from Platte County, are you?

HEAD WRITER

You are all nuts! We're going to lose this account. How about you, Robert? You got something? Anything?

The camera pans down the table. We see Bob Warhammer at the opposite end of the table.

BOB WARHAMMER

I got nothin'.

Silence. Head Writer puts his face in his hands. Writer 1, Writer 2, Writer 3 and Writer 4 stare at Bob Warhammer.

Fade out.

Medium Coffee The Medium

═══

FADE IN

INT. - THEATER

We see man sitting in a chair at a low table. On the table is a coffee cup with the word "Medium" on it.

KYLE MCINTYRE

(In a deep radio voice.) Good evening! My name is Kyle McIntyre. Welcome to Communication From Beyond, the show that welcomes psychics, mediums, clairvoyants, and those with the gift of ESP. Tonight's guest is one I've been anxious to have on this program for some time – Medium Coffee the Medium. Welcome to the show, Medium Coffee!

MEDIUM COFFEE THE MEDIUM

Thank you, Kyle. It's good to be here.

KYLE MCINTYRE

For those of our audience who are unfamiliar with your work, you are an actual medium cup of coffee.

MEDIUM COFFEE THE MEDIUM

That's right, Kyle, a full 16 ounces.

KYLE MCINTYRE

And yet, you are a medium.

MEDIUM COFFEE THE MEDIUM

That's right, Kyle. With the help of my spirit guides, I can communicate with cups of coffee that have crossed over.

KYLE MCINTYRE

And when did you first realize you had this gift?

MEDIUM COFFEE THE MEDIUM

Kyle, if you don't mind, I'm getting several messages from my spirit guides and I'd like to get started with a reading right now.

KYLE MCINTYRE

By all means.

MEDIUM COFFEE THE MEDIUM

I'm getting a strong message from a venti Frappuccino with soy milk. I know that's not very specific. Now I'm getting a name that starts with a hard "C" or a "K." Carol? Connie? Katherine? I'm seeing the number "8." Is there a Kate in the audience?

KATE

Yes?

MEDIUM COFFEE THE MEDIUM

Kate? A venti Frappuccino, with soy milk, is that right?

KATE

Yes! I can't believe this!

MEDIUM COFFEE THE MEDIUM

Clearly you were at a Starbucks. I'm being shown a bullseye. Was that Starbucks in a Target?

KATE

Yes! Oh my god! I loved that cup of coffee. I can't believe it remembered me!

MEDIUM COFFEE THE MEDIUM

You were there to buy a blouse. Wait. You bought a blouse? A red blouse?

KATE

Yes! (Kate fans herself.)

MEDIUM COFFEE THE MEDIUM

And even though it didn't quite fit quite right, you knew it would after you dropped those 30 pounds you've been trying to shed.

KATE

Heh-heh… What?

MEDIUM COFFEE THE MEDIUM

And you were wearing those unfortunate slacks and a sweater that looked like it came from the dollar bin at the Salvation Army.

KATE

(Angry) What??? I love that sweater! What is wrong with you?

MEDIUM COFFEE THE MEDIUM

Oh, you're starting to fade. I think I'm getting another message. Let's see - a large dark roast - at a convenience store. I wish I could be more specific. I'm seeing a "Q". A QuikTrip? Yes. I believe it's a QuikTrip. For Will or William. Willy? Bill? Billy?

BILLY

That could be me.

MEDIUM COFFEE THE MEDIUM

Let's make sure I have the right person. I'm seeing a calendar. On the weekend, right?

BILLY

Right.

MEDIUM COFFEE THE MEDIUM

Every weekend? Wait. Every Saturday?

BILLY

Yeah, that's me. Pretty much every Saturday morning. Who told you?

MEDIUM COFFEE THE MEDIUM

Two sugars, right?

BILLY

No, that's not me.

MEDIUM COFFEE THE MEDIUM

I'm being shown two sugars.

BILLY

I can't have sugar. Doctor's orders.

MEDIUM COFFEE THE MEDIUM

Let me make sure. You were wearing a green baseball cap. With a deer? A John Deere baseball cap? Is that right?

BILLY

Well, sure, but I don't think that's me.

MEDIUM COFFEE THE MEDIUM

And you were wearing your 2015 Royals World Series t-shirt, black steel-toed work boots, and a Kansas City Chiefs belt buckle?

BILLY

(Angry) Hey, look! If a guy can't enjoy a cup of coffee on the weekends, what's this world... You know what? Screw you and the coffee pot you rode in on. The coffee pot you rode in in.

KYLE MCINTYRE

Medium Coffee, I think we have time for one more.

MEDIUM COFFEE THE MEDIUM

Aright. I'm seeing Folger's in someone's favorite coffee cup. It's coming from this part of the audience. It's a "J" name, or a soft "G". Georgianna? Jordan? No. Josephine? Josie?

JOSIE

Yes?

MEDIUM COFFEE THE MEDIUM

Josie? You were having a cup of coffee in a special cup in someone's kitchen. Someone you love.

JOSIE

That's right. Now I'm getting nervous.

MEDIUM COFFEE THE MEDIUM

I see a female figure above... an aunt? Your mother? Your grandmother?

JOSIE

Oh my God, yes!

MEDIUM COFFEE THE MEDIUM

Don't say any more. I'm being shown an empty coffee cup. Wait. Has she recently passed?

JOSIE

Yes, just last week. Is she here now? (Starts to cry.) I love you, Grandma!

MEDIUM COFFEE THE MEDIUM

Yes, she's here now, and she's showing me roses, which means she sends her love to you. Wait. Now I'm being shown a microphone. Who is Mike?

JOSIE

My boyfriend. Grandma, I miss you so much!

MEDIUM COFFEE THE MEDIUM

I'm being shown M&Ms. Did your grandmother like M&Ms?

JOSIE

No, I don't think so.

MEDIUM COFFEE THE MEDIUM

I'm being shown M&Ms. Now I'm getting a statue of the Virgin Mary. Who is Mary?

JOSIE

That's his old girlfriend.

MEDIUM COFFEE THE MEDIUM

Ok. That explains the M&Ms. Your grandmother is showing M and M together.

JOSIE

No, they broke up.

MEDIUM COFFEE THE MEDIUM

No, they're together. Now I'm being shown something bad... something nasty. Did your grandmother call it "doing the nasty"?

JOSIE

Yes. Why?

MEDIUM COFFEE THE MEDIUM

Your grandmother says M and M are doing the nasty right now.

JOSIE

(Upset) What?

MEDIUM COFFEE THE MEDIUM

Yes, that's very clear. Now she's showing me Mike has warrants out for his arrest.

JOSIE

(Angry) What???

MEDIUM COFFEE THE MEDIUM

One in Florida for fleeing the scene of an accident and a bench warrant in Tennessee for failure to appear at a court-ordered urinalysis.

JOSIE

(Irate) That son of a bitch! I'm going to kick his ass!

KYLE MCINTYRE

This has been amazing, but I'm afraid we're out of time. Thank you so much for joining us today, Medium Coffee.

MEDIUM COFFEE THE MEDIUM

It's been my pleasure, but I believe I'm getting a message for you, Kyle. From a cappuccino...

KYLE MCINTYRE

I'm sorry, Medium Coffee, we're out of time.

MEDIUM COFFEE THE MEDIUM

. . . at an out-of-the-way bistro. . .

KYLE MCINTYRE

I wish we had more time. Ladies and gentlemen, thank you for joining us for another episode of the show that welcomes psychics, mediums, clairvoyants, and those with the gift of ESP.

MEDIUM COFFEE THE MEDIUM

Oh! And you're not alone!

KYLE MCINTYRE

(Angry) Shut up! (Resumes his radio voice.) Be sure to join us next time on Communication From Beyond.

Fade out.

Me and Yuh

FADE IN.

1 INT. BANK.

CUSTOMER walks up to a teller, who has a name plate "Ms. Yuh."

MS. YUH

Can I help you?

CUSTOMER

I sure hope so. My Aunt Helen has Alzheimer's. I was helping her with some legal papers, and said to her, "Just sign your name on that line." So, she signed it "Your Name."

MS. YUH

My name?

CUSTOMER

No, no. She signed it (CUSTOMER mimics signing a form) "Your." "Name."

MS. YUH

Oh, no! Did it all get taken care of?

CUSTOMER

Yes, but it was a mess. Recently, she wanted write me a check, and asked me how to make it out. I said, "Just make it out to me." So she made it out to "Me."

MS. YUH

Do you have an account at this bank?

CUSTOMER

Yes.

MS. YUH

Then just sign the back of the check.

CUSTOMER

See, that's the problem. My signature won't match the name on the check.

MS. YUH

Who's it made out to?

CUSTOMER

"Me."

MS. YUH

So it shouldn't be a problem.

CUSTOMER

I'm pretty sure it will.

MS. YUH

Why?

CUSTOMER

Well, doesn't the signature on the back of the check have to match the name on the front of the check?

MS. YUH

Yes.

CUSTOMER

Then they won't match.

MS. YUH

I don't understand. Let me see the check. Oh, my goodness! I see what you're talking about. The check's made out to "Me."

CUSTOMER

(Smiles) No, it's made out to me.

MS. YUH

(Smiles) That's what I said.

CUSTOMER

No, you said it was made out to you.

MS. YUH

If it had been made out to "Yuh," it would have my name on it.

CUSTOMER

What?

MS. YUH

And I could sign the back and cash it.

CUSTOMER

Wait. Didn't you just say it was made out to you?

MS. YUH

No, I said if it were made out to "Yuh," then I could sign the back and cash it.

CUSTOMER

What???

MS. YUH

(Pointing to the name plate.) Because my name is "Yuh." (Laughs.)

CUSTOMER

(Laughs.) Oh, I get it. Wow, that's confusing. Have you thought about changing your name?

MS. YUH

Funny you should say that. I'm getting married next week.

CUSTOMER

Congratulations. What's the name of your fiancé?

MS. YUH

William Noh.

CUSTOMER

No?

MS. YUH

Yes.

CUSTOMER

So it's Noh?

MS. YUH

Yes. When he asked me, I said, "Yes."

CUSTOMER

I know.

MS. YUH

No, not I Noh. William Noh. Have you met him?

CUSTOMER

No.

MS. YUH

Yes. Have you met him?

CUSTOMER

No.

MS. YUH

That's right. William Noh. Have you met him?

CUSTOMER

I don't think so. Do you think you'll change your name when you marry?

MS. YUH

Maybe. But here's the thing. My first initial is "I."

CUSTOMER

And?

MS. YUH

If I use my first initial, then my new name would be "I. Noh."

CUSTOMER

What?

MS. YUH

I. Noh.

CUSTOMER

Well, I should hope so. You're the one getting married.

MS. YUH

What?

CUSTOMER

You said, "I know."

MS. YUH

That would be my new name. (Ms. Yuh mimics writing.) I. Noh.

CUSTOMER

(Laughing) Oh, I get it. That's confusing.

MS. YUH

Yes, but I'm thinking about about using my middle name, too. It's Wanda.

CUSTOMER

So your new name would be...

MS. YUH

I Wanda Noh.

CUSTOMER

You want to know?

MS. YUH

No, not U. Wanda Noh. I Wanda Noh.

CUSTOMER

You do?

MS. YUH

What?

CUSTOMER

Wanna know.

MS. YUH

No, I said (demonstrating) I. Wanda. Noh. Which can be confusing.

CUSTOMER

No kidding! I'm confused! (Laughs.)

MS. NOH

Or I may hyphenate my new name.

CUSTOMER

So then your name would be…

MS. YUH

Yuh-Noh.

CUSTOMER

No, I don't. Tell me.

MS. YUH

Tell me what?

CUSTOMER

Your new name.

MS. YUH

Yuh-Noh.

CUSTOMER

No, I won't until you tell me.

MS. YUH

(Mimics writing.) Yuh. Hyphen. Noh.

CUSTOMER

(Smililng) Oh, I get it. It looks like your name will be confusing no matter what you decide. Look, this is all very interesting, but what I really want to do is cash this check.

MS. YUH

I don't think I can help you. Do you want me to get a manager?

CUSTOMER

That's a great idea.

The MANAGER walks by.

MS. NOH

Oh, I'm glad you walked by. Can you help us?

MANAGER

If I can. What's the problem?

CUSTOMER

I'm trying to cash a check, but it's made out to "Me."

MANAGER

Do you have an account with the bank?

CUSTOMER

Yes.

MANAGER

Then just sign the back of the check.

CUSTOMER

That won't work.

MS. YUH

We've been over this. Here's why we need your help. (She hands the Manager the check.)

MANAGER

Aha! It's made out to "Me."

CUSTOMER

(Smiling) But it's supposed to be made out to me.

MANAGER

That's what I said.

MS. YUH

We've been through this. For a while, we thought it was made out to "Yuh."

MANAGER

What made you think it was made out to me?

CUSTOMER

Not you. (CUSTOMER points to MS. YUH.) Her.

MANAGER

I never said it was made out to her.

MS. YUH

(To Manager) If it were made out to Yuh, I could cash it.

CUSTOMER

Exactly.

MANAGER

What???

CUSTOMER

(To Manager) But it's not made out to (pointing) you or (pointing) Yuh. It's made out to (points to self) me.

MS. YUH

Right. I told him "Just sign your name on the back."

CUSTOMER

But my aunt Helen tried that once, and it caused problems.

MANAGER

It caused problems when she signed her name?

CUSTOMER

Not her name. "Your name."

MANAGER

How did she know my name?

MS. YUH

She has Alzheimer's.

MS.YUH and CUSTOMER nod their heads.

MANAGER

What??

CUSTOMER

She has Alzheimer's.

MANAGER

That doesn't explain how she knew my name. Unless she's clairvoyant.

CUSTOMER

What makes you think her name is Claire Voyant?

MANAGER

What?

CUSTOMER

Her name's not Claire. It's Helen. My Aunt Helen.

MANAGER

I know.

MS. YUH

Actually, that might be my name after I get married.

MANAGER

After you get married, your name will be "Aunt Helen?"

MS. YUH

Actually, I haven't decided. It might be Yuh-Noh.

MANAGER

It might be what?

MS. YUH

Yuh-Noh.

MANAGER

No, I don't.

CUSTOMER

Look. We've been through this. My aunt was confused. That's why she signed "Your Name."

MS. YUH

(To the Manager) And because she signed "Your Name," she got in trouble.

MANAGER

Of course. The bank has rules.

CUSTOMER

Exactly! That's why I don't know how to cash this check!

MANAGER

Listen. Just sign the check.

CUSTOMER

What?

MANAGER

Just sign your name on the back.

CUSTOMER

(Using air quotes) "Your name"?

MANAGER

No, (points to CUSTOMER) your name.

MS. YUH

That won't work. We just explained that his aunt tried that and it got her in trouble. Remember her? The one you wanted to call "Clair?"

MANAGER

Listen. You should sign the back.

MS. YUH

(Smiling) Me?

MANAGER

No, not you. (Pointing to the CUSTOMER) You!

CUSTOMER

Look. This is going nowhere. Thanks for trying to help, but I think I'd better write a letter to the President of the bank, and ask his opinion. To be clear, what's your name?

MANAGER

Roger N. Dorsitt.

CUSTOMER

Roger what?

MANAGER

N. Dorsitt.

CUSTOMER

That's what I've been trying to do!

All three start talking at once.

Fade out.

Baseball and Shakespeare

———

FADE IN.

1 INT – THE OFFICE OF THE ATHLETIC DIRECTOR

The Athletic Director, BIFF BRINDLEMEYER, is wearing a Park University sweatshirt and sweatpants. He has a whistle around his neck. He's on the phone.

BIFF BRINDLEMEYER

Tell the coach we wish him a speedy recovery. And please let us know when he'll be well enough to have visitors. Ok... ok... please take care.

He hangs up as STUDENT ASSISTANT walks into the office, looking at his phone. STUDENT ASSISTANT is wearing a Park University t-shirt and khakis.

BIFF BRINDLEMEYER

Well, we're screwed.

STUDENT ASSISTANT

(He looks up from his phone.) What's wrong?

BIFF BRINDLEMEYER

Coach Wellspring was in an accident. Some little darlin' on a cell phone ran a stop sign and t-boned him. He's had surgery and is in intensive care.

STUDENT ASSISTANT

Oh, no! Is he going to be all right?

BIFF BRINDLEMEYER

Yeah, probably, but he's going to be laid up for quite a while. This really sucks for us. Baseball tryouts start in a couple of weeks, and now I don't have a coach!

STUDENT ASSISTANT

(Working his phone.) Hold on. Wait. Did you know we have a new coach on faculty this semester?

BIFF BRINDLEMEYER

A new coach? What? Who? Why wasn't I told about this?

STUDENT ASSISTANT

(Looking at his phone.) It's an acting coach. SIR CEDRIC Shortfellow. He's on loan from University of Westchestershire, England.

BIFF BRINDLEMEYER

Hey, a coach is a coach. Let's go talk to him.

STUDENT ASSISTANT

Seriously?

BIFF BRINDLEMEYER

Yeah! Come on! Let's go! Hustle! (BIFF BRINDLEMEYER blows his whistle. STUDENT ASSISTANT runs out, with BIFF BRINDLEMEYER walking behind.) Go! Go! Move it!

2 INT – A STAGE

SIR CEDRIC is dressed in Elizabethan costume, as he is in every scene. He holds a copy of Hamlet in his hand, gesturing to an invisible audience. BIFF BRINDLEMEYER and STUDENT ASSISTANT approach SIR CEDRIC from off stage.

SIR CEDRIC

(Overacting. SIR CEDRIC always overacts.) But soft! What light through yonder window breaks? It is the east, and Juliet is the sun. Arise, fair sun, and kill the envious moon who is already sick and pale with grief that thou, her maid, art far more fair than she.

BIFF BRINDLEMEYER

Hey, coach! I'm BIFF BRINDLEMEYER, Athletic Director. I don't think we've met. (BIFF BRINDLEMEYER reaches out to shake SIR CEDRIC's hand.)

SIR CEDRIC

(SIR CEDRIC ignores the hand and bows instead.) Or call it winter, which being full of care, makes summer's welcome, thrice more wished, more rare.

BIFF BRINDLEMEYER

(To STUDENT ASSISTANT) What'd he say?

STUDENT ASSISTANT

He said, "Glad to meet you."

BIFF BRINDLEMEYER

(To STUDENT ASSISTANT) You sure he's a coach?

STUDENT ASSISTANT

(Looking at his phone) Yes. It's on the university website.
(STUDENT ASSISTANT shows his phone to BIFF
BRINDLEMEYER. BIFF BRINDLEMEYER ignores it.)

SIR CEDRIC

Pray, what brings you to these hallowed boards?

BIFF BRINDLEMEYER

I don't know if you heard, but Coach Wellspring won't be able to
coach the baseball team this spring. Is there any chance you'd be
interested in taking over for one season?

SIR CEDRIC

What say you? To coach not for the stage, but for the field of ball and
base? To travail to raise in victory the flag of the Park Pirates? But
hold... pirates? Who stand in polar opposition to all that is fair and
pure? Pirates? Scourge of the seven seas? Sworn enemies of his
majesty's galleons? But... what's in a name? A rose by any other name
smells just as sweet! So... sound drums and trumpets! Raise the flag of
bones and skull! Let the house of gold and wine emerge victorious
from the fray! Ha-ha!!!

BIFF BRINDLEMEYER

(Whispering to STUDENT ASSISTANT) What'd he say?

STUDENT ASSISTANT

(Looking at his phone.) He said he'd do it.

BIFF BRINDLEMEYER

(To SIR CEDRIC) Great! Thanks, coach! (He takes SIR CEDRIC's
hand and shakes it vigorously. He drops SIR CEDRIC's hand and

thrusts his fist in the air.) GO, PIRATES! WOO-HOO! (Turns to STUDENT ASSISTANT.) Ok, mission accomplished. Let's go! (BIFF BRINDLEMEYER blows his whistle. STUDENT ASSISTANT runs off stage, with BIFF BRINDLEMEYER walking behind.) Move it! Go! Go!

3 EXT – A COURTYARD ON CAMPUS

SIR CEDRIC and STUDENT ASSISTANT walk to the middle of the courtyard. A number of students are walking by, looking at their phones. When SIR CEDRIC starts talking, they stop and look up.

SIR CEDRIC

Friends, Pirates, countrymen, lend me your ears! I have come in search of players for the Park University Ball and Base Spring Festival. Readings for the various roles shall occur within the fortnight. Doubt thou the stars are fire, doubt that the sun doth move, doubt that truth be a liar, but never doubt that I shall treasure leading the cast on this noble quest. (Bows)

The students stare at SIR CEDRIC. STUDENT ASSISTANT steps forward.

STUDENT ASSISTANT

SIR CEDRIC will be our baseball coach this year. Tryouts will be next week.

The students stare at STUDENT ASSISTANT.

I've posted it on the Athletic Department web site.

The students look at their phones, nod and walk away.

4 INT – OUTSIDE A CLASSROOM

We see a bulletin board outside a classroom. A parchment, labeled "Callback List" is pinned to it.

Call Back Liste

- **Base the first:**
  - Cy Dwahk
  - Stan Doffish
- **Base the second:**
  - Ray Zinell
  - Neal Don DuPrey
- **Base the third:**
  - Eubie deJudge
  - E. Rex Karrs
- **Short Stoppe:**
  - James Johnson
  - Ben Zadrine
- **Catchers:**
  - Alan A. Dazewerk
  - Dewitt R. Else
- **Upstage players:**
  - Moe deLaun
  - Les Wurk
  - Lou Brakk
  - Paul Bearer
  - Robin Banks
- **Leads:**
  - Miles Peraur
  - Saul Tenpepper
  - Tom Maytoe
  - Eubie deJudge

The camera pulls back to show a group of students, some wearing Park University baseball caps. The students are reading the Callback Liste. A few students walk away, disappointed. The rest enter the classroom.

5 INT - CLASSROOM

SIR CEDRIC stands at the front of the classroom. STUDENT ASSISTANT faces the classroom, sitting at a computer. There is a screen behind them.

SIR CEDRIC

Welcome, players! My love of the game is mine to teach, and all shalt see how apt thou art to learn. I commend your attention to the following matter. (SIR CEDRIC nods to STUDENT ASSISTANT.)

6 THE POWERPOINT PRESENTATION

We see the Slide 1, which is the outline of a baseball diamond. The infield is labeled "Downstage," the outfield is labeled "Upstage," left field is labeled "Stage Right," right field is labeled "Stage Left," and center field is labeled "Centre Stage."

SIR CEDRIC (Voice Over)

The field of play, that is, the stage hath two components: Upstage and Downstage. Upstage hath three components: Stage Right, Centre Stage and Stage Left. Next slide.

We see Slide 2, which is the outline of the infield. The pitching mound is labeled "The Lead," the batter's box is labeled "The Antagonist," the on deck circle is labeled "Waiting in the Wings," and the area below home plate is labeled "The Critic."

SIR CEDRIC (Voice Over)

Downstage is in truth the main stage of the production, for much of the joy, suspense and agony of the play transpires therein. The lines are delivered by the lead to the antagonist who struggles mightily to respond. In the wings is the next player awaiting his cue to enter the stage. All is observed and judged by the critic, whose opinion, though frequently and vociferously challenged, is law.

7 INT - CLASSROOM

SIR CEDRIC

And now, Farewell! Thou art too dear for my possessing, and like enough thou knowest thy estimate. Thus have I had thee as a dream doth flatter: In sleep a king, but waking no such matter. (Bows)

The players stare at SIR CEDRIC. STUDENT ASSISTANT stands up.

STUDENT ASSISTANT

That's it. Practice tomorrow at 4:00, sharp. (The players stare at STUDENT ASSISTANT.) I posted a meeting notification on the university website so you can add it to your calendars.

The players look at their phones, nod, stand and move toward the door.

8 EXT – THE STANDS AT PARK UNIVSERSITY'S COMFORT FIELD

BIFF BRINDLEMEYER and STUDENT ASSISTANT are in the front row. STUDENT ASSISTANT is looking at his phone.

BIFF BRINDLEMEYER

I love opening day! This is going to be great! You couldn't ask for a prettier day!

STUDENT ASSISTANT

(Looking at his phone.) There's a storm front moving in. Should be here in a couple of hours.

BIFF BRINDLEMEYER

(Sarcastically.) As long as you're on your phone, why don't you look up "buzzkill"?

STUDENT ASSISTANT

(Talking to his phone.) Siri, what is buzzkill?

BIFF BRINDLEMEYER

Seriously?

VOICE FROM OFF CAMERA

Hey, brainy boy! The coach needs you!

BIFF BRINDLEMEYER

You heard him. (Blows his whistle.) Go! Move it! Move it! (STUDENT ASSISTANT runs off camera.)

9 EXT – THE DUGOUT AT PARK UNIVSERSITY'S COMFORT FIELD

Players are warming up. STUDENT ASSISTANT and SIR CEDRIC stand together. SIR CEDRIC is wearing his Elizabethan outfit and a Park University baseball cap. STUDENT ASSISTANT is looking at his phone.

SIR CEDRIC

Good players, a moment! (The players gather.) I see you stand like greyhounds in the slips, straining upon the start. The game's afoot: follow your spirit, and upon this charge stiffen the sinews, summon up the blood. But be thou mindful. There be players that I have seen play, that having neither the accent of Pirates, nor the gait of Pirates, who have so strutted and bellowed that I have thought some of Nature's journeymen had made them, and not made them well, they imitated humanity so abominably. In victory there's nothing so becomes a man as modest stillness and humility. Now, once more unto the breach, dear friends! To honor! To victory! To university!

The players look confused. STUDENT ASSISTANT looks up from his phone and steps forward.

STUDENT ASSISTANT

Be good sports. Make Park University proud. Go, Pirates.

(The players nod, then return to warming up.)

10 EXT – A BROADCAST BOOTH

BROADCASTER 1

Bottom of the first, one out. Johnson steps in and taps the plate. Here's the pitch.

UMPIRE (Voice over)

Strike!

BROADCASTER 1

A knee-high slider. The count is 0 and 1. Wait a minute! Coach Shortfellow is going out to home plate. I wonder what this is about.

11 EXT – HOME PLATE

SIR CEDRIC strides into the scene. The umpire takes off his mask.

SIR CEDRIC

What, anon? Do mine ears, my loyal and faithful companions for lo, these many years, now turn to distrust and deceit? For they hear a call of "Strike," when clearly, the pitch was low. Were the player not standing, but rather kneeling, as in a prayer box, begging forgiveness for past errors, then and then alone would the call would be justly so.

HOME PLATE UMPIRE

Coach! Coach! Wait a minute! The coach can't argue balls and strikes. You'll have to go back to the bench.

SIR CEDRIC

What say you? Very well! When in Rome, I shall do as the Romans. I take my leave, but not willingly do I go. Good day to you, squire!

SIR CEDRIC strides off camera.

12 EXT – THE STANDS

We see BIFF BRINDLEMEYER and STUDENT ASSISTANT. STUDENT ASSISTANT is looking at his phone.

BIFF BRINDLEMEYER

(To the STUDENT ASSISTANT) What'd he say?

STUDENT ASSISTANT

(Without looking up from his phone.) He said, "You missed the call."

BIFF BRINDLEMEYER

Oh... ok. (Yelling at the umpire) Come on, blue! Open your eyes! Go,
Pirates! Woo-hoo!

13 EXT – BROADCAST BOOTH

BROADCASTER 1

This could be the game, fans. It's the bottom of the eighth with the
score tied 2-2. Park has runners on first and third with only one out.
The infield is drawn in.

BROADCASTER 2

Lots of ways to score here. I wonder what the coach will dial up.

14 EXT – THE DUGOUT

SIR CEDRIC paces back and forth behind the bench. SIR CEDRIC
stops pacing.

SIR CEDRIC

To squeeze, or not to squeeze, that is the question. Whether 'tis nobler
in the mind to suffer the slings and arrows of a catcher blocking the
plate, or to take arms against a sea of troubles, and by opposing slide
under the tag. To win, to lose, perchance to dream. Ay, there's the rub.
For in that sleep of loss, what dreams may come when we have shuffled
off this dusty field must give us pause. (SIR CEDRIC resumes
pacing.)

15 EXT – THE STANDS

STUDENT   ASSISTANT   is   looking   at   his   phone.   BIFF
BRINDLEMEYER turns to STUDENT ASSISTANT.

BIFF BRINDLEMEYER

What'd he say?

STUDENT ASSISTANT

(Without looking up from his phone.) Well, he can't make up his mind whether or not to bunt, so we're going to swing away.

BIFF BRINDLEMEYER

Ok, thanks. (To the field.) C'mon, boys! Ducks on the pond! Go, Pirates! Woo-hoo!

16 EXT – THE BROADCAST BOOTH

BROADCASTER 1

What a way to start the season! The Pirates win in a thriller, 3-2, scoring the winning run on a timely hit in the bottom of the eighth.

BROADCASTER 2

This should make our new coach proud. High fives all around. Hey, wait a minute. What's going on? The players are lining up on the first base line. What is this?

17 EXT – COMFORT FIELD

Players are lined up on first-base line facing the stands. They reach down, grab each other's hands, and do a curtain call. The fans can be heard cheering off camera.

18 EXT – THE BROADCAST BOOTH

BROADCASTER 1

Let's see if Park can continue its impressive five-game win streak. Top of the third, one out, Johnson on first. One ball, one strike on Wilson.

BROADCASTER 2

JIMMY JOHNSON already has four stolen bases this year. Let's see if he goes.

BROADCASTER 1

Johnson takes his lead. There he goes! Here's the pitch. The pitch is outside, here's the throw.

SECOND BASE UMPIRE (voice over)

You're out!

BROADCASTER 1

They got him! Close call!

BROADCASTER 2

You know it would take a good throw to get Johnson, and that throw was right on the bag! Johnson can't believe it!

BROADCASTER 1

Wait a minute! Time out! Coach Shortfellow is walking toward second base.

19 EXT – SECOND BASE

The Second Base Umpire stands behind the bag, hands on his hips. JIMMY JOHNSON is upset. He's looking at the Second Base Umpire in disbelief. SIR CEDRIC walks into the scene.

SIR CEDRIC

Now is the winter of my discontent with all the clouds that lour'd upon our team. For with wonder I look and what do I see? A fist thrust into the air? Oh... 'tis a vision most foul. Hast thou not seen foot and base? Glove and tag? Ohhhh.... 'tis a tale told by an idiot! Full of sound and fury, and signifying nothing!

JIMMY JOHNSON trots off. SIR CEDRIC starts walking back to the bench. We hear applause from the stands.

FANS (Voice over)

"Bravo!" "Huzzah" "Encore!"

SIR CEDRIC stops and bows with a flourish.

SIR CEDRIC

Thank you! Thank you so much! You are too kind!

20 EXT – BROADCAST BOOTH

BROADCASTER 1

That concludes the American Midwest Conference tournament for your Park Pirates. They win the consolation game 7-3 to finish third in the conference.

BROADCASTER 2

What a season for our Pirates! Pre-season polls had them finishing in the bottom half of the league, but they came out of nowhere to finish 19-7. I'll bet there will be a lot of proud Pirate moms and dads at the banquet! That's it for today, fans. This is KGSP-FM, 90.5-FM.

21 INT – BANQUET HALL

A long table and podium. Behind the table is a Park University banner. Announcer 1 and Announcer 2 are seated at the table. BIFF BRINDLEMEYER stands at the podium, still wearing his Park

University sweatshirt, sweatpants and a whistle. Next to him is STUDENT ASSISTANT, looking at his phone. Off to one side is SIR CEDRIC.

BIFF BRINDLEMEYER

(Reading from a script.) To conclude, let me thank you again for attending tonight, and for your continued support of the Park University Pirates baseball program. And a special thanks to Coach Sir Cedric Shortfellow for filling in this season. What a job! (Polite applause from the audience.) Now, players, if you will walk across the stage one at a time to get your trophy, then get a special document from Coach Shortfellow. First, Jimmy Johnson, our all-conference shortstop! (Blows whistle.) C'mon! Move it!

JIMMY JOHNSON walks across the stage, gets a trophy from BIFF BRINDLEMEYER, shakes his hand, then continues and gets a parchment from SIR CEDRIC. He stops and looks at the parchment, then looks up.

JIMMY JOHNSON

Hey, everybody! We get three credit hours in Theater! Wow! Thanks coach!

We hear players cheering. JIMMY JOHNSON takes a bow with a flourish, much like SIR CEDRIC did, earlier. They hold hands and do a curtain call.

THE AUDIENCE (Voice over)

Bravo! Bravo! Huzzah!

Fade out.

A New TV Show

FADE IN.

1 INT – CONFERENCE ROOM

Seated at a large table are four writers and HEAD WRITER.

HEAD WRITER

As you know, we're trying to create a new TV show. This is the first stage – listening to proposals for pilots. You've had a few days to come up with something. What have you got?

WRITER 1

I call this pilot "CSI Cartagena." I'll be interested to get your reactions. Picture this. It's another hot, humid summer day in Cartagena. The camera shows on the exterior of a back alley hole-in-the-wall bar.

2 INT – BACK-ALLEY BAR - DAY

WRITER 1 (Voice over)

Inside, the camera reveals a close-up of a dusty ceiling fan, slowing slowly rotating.

HEAD WRITER (Voice over)

Good start. Go on.

WRITER 1 (Voice over)

The camera pulls back revealing red twine hanging from the fan. A twine is tied around one blade of the fan – a twine usually found wrapped around deliveries of cocaine.

The purpose of the twine is revealed as the camera continues to pull back, revealing a slowly-rotating corpse in a noose that's made of twine.

The camera continues to pull back, revealing the corpse's intestines, which are dangling from the body. The intestines make obscene circles in his blood which has pooled beneath him on the floor.

The continues to camera pull back. It has been looking over the shoulders of two men.

A Police Captain and his Lieutenant survey the scene. They stare at the corpse, unmoving. They seem to be frozen in time. Finally, one of them speaks.

LIEUTENANT

What do you think, Captain? Another suicide?

WRITER 1 (Voice over)

The Captain slowly looks up, then down, the left and right. He removes a cigarette from his mouth before speaking.

CAPTAIN

Well, Lieutenent, it sure looks like it.

3 INT – BOARD ROOM

HEAD WRITER

At first glance, this seems disturbingly racist and offensively stereotypical. Well, everyone, what do you think?

The camera pans down the table. Writer 1 is smiling. Writer 2 and Writer 3 are shaking their heads. Finally, we see Writer 4, who is wearing a wide-rimmed Mexican hat and a brightly-colored poncho.

WRITER 4

I think I have an idea that will make this a go. How about this?

4 INT – BACK-ALLEY BAR - DAY

WRITER 4 (Voice over)

The camera moves back. It has been looking over the shoulders of the two men.

LIEUTENANT

What do you think, Captain? Another suicide?

WRITER 4 (Voice over)

The Captain slowly looks up, then down, the left and right. He removes a cigarette from his mouth before speaking.

CAPTAIN

Well, Lieutenant, it sure looks like it.

LIEUTENANT

Great! Hey, tequilas, everyone?

WRITER 4 (Voice over)

They all begin dancing, and start to form a conga line. More police join them. A guitar band appears, people put on big straw hats, and a celebration ensues.

5 INT – BOARD ROOM

They stare at Writer 4 in disbelief. Writer 4 smiles and nods.

HEAD WRITER

How about this? NO! Absolutely not! Anyone else?

WRITER 2

Check this out. I call this "The Bachelor – Saudi Arabia."

6 INT – STAGE

WRITER 2 (Voice over)

The camera shows a world map. It slowly zooms in on the Arabian Peninsula, then Saudi Arabia, then Riyadh. Cut to an interior shot of a stage with a number of women in burkas. All we can see of their faces is their eyes.

The camera moves down the row of six women.

HEAD WRITER (Voice over)

I like it so far. How many women?

WRITER 2 (Voice over)

I don't know. Say, four.

Two women leave.

WRITER 2 (Voice over)

Off to the side, we see an announcer with a microphone. Next to him is a handsome Arab man wearing the traditional white dishdasha robe and a turbin.

HOST

It's been four weeks, Prince Khalid. You've dated each of these lovely young women in turn, accompanied at all times by her parents and the producers of this show. Here's a rose. The world awaits your decision. With which of these lovely bachelorettes do you choose to spend the rest of your life?"

Prince Khalid slowly scans the room, twisting the rose in his hands. He gestures with the rose in a sweeping motion.

PRINCE KHALID

I choose all of them.

HOST

Well, there you have it, ladies and gentlemen! Be sure to join us next time for another episode of The Bachelor, Saudi Arabia!

7 INT – BOARD ROOM

HEAD WRITER

I'm not sure. Well, everyone, what do you think?

The camera pans down the table. Writer 1 and Writer 3 shake their heads. Writer 2 is smiling. Finally, we see Writer 4.

WRITER 4

I think I have an idea that will make this a go. How about this?

8 INT – STAGE

HOST

With which of these lovely bachelorettes do you choose to spend the rest of your life?"

Prince Khalid slowly scans the room, twisting the rose in his hands. He gestures with the rose in a sweeping motion.

PRINCE KHALID

I choose all of them.

HOST

Well, there you have it, ladies and gentlemen! Be sure to join us next time for another episode of The Bachelor, Saudi Arabia! Hey, tequilas, everyone?

They all break into a dance and start to form a conga line. The two extra women join them. A guitar band appears, people put on big straw hats, and a celebration ensues. Fade out.

9 INT – BOARD ROOM

Silence. They stare at Writer 4 in disbelief. Writer 4 smiles and nods.

HEAD WRITER

Have you lost your mind? Anyone else?

WRITER 3

Okay. I call this pilot "To Kill a Mockingbird, Orange Valley." Check this out.

10 INT – STAGE

WRITER 3 (Voice over)

The scene is a small courtroom. The camera shows the table of the accused, a poor Mexican laborer, who sits with slumped shoulders. His left hand is on the table. His right hand is motionless in his lap. He stares at the table in front of him. His Defense Attorney leans over to whisper something to him. The man nods his head.

HEAD WRITER (Voice over)

I think I've seen this movie.

WRITER 3 (Voice over)

Just wait. The camera slowly turns to show the table where the prosecutor sits. He is leaning back, smiling confidently. The camera pans across the jury box. Many jurors are fanning themselves and staring at the accused. One is working a crossword puzzle. A young woman is chewing gum, and staring at her phone. The camera continues to turn to reveal the bailiff standing next to a desk. The camera continues to pan to reveal an elevated platform holding a desk with a gavel on it. Behind the desk is a leather chair.

BAILIFF

All rise!

The judge enters through a door to one side, and sits in the leather chair.

BAILIFF

You may be seated.

JUDGE

Counselors, shall we begin?

DEFENSE ATTORNEY

Your honor, may I approach?

The judge nods. The defense attorney approaches the desk. He speaks loudly enough for everyone to hear.

DEFENSE ATTORNEY

Your honor, my client is innocent. The evidence clearly shows that the crime was committed by a right-handed person, and my client lost the use of his right arm ten years ago in an agricultural accident. I move for dismissal.

The camera shows the accused. He looks up and, using his left hand, lifts his right arm and lets it fall on the table. The judge looks at the accused, then at the Defense Attorney, then picks up a paper from the desk and stares at it.

JUDGE

Fair enough. Case dismissed. (He bangs the gavel.)

11 INT – BOARD ROOM

HEAD WRITER

That's it? That's the best you can do? Pathetic. Seriously?

The camera pans down the table. Writer 1 and Writer 2 shake their heads. Writer 3 is smiling. Finally, we see Writer 4.

WRITER 4

I think I have an idea that will make this a go.

HEAD WRITER

No! Absolutely not! Another "Tequilas, everyone?" Are you kidding me? Forget it.

WRITER 4

No, no. Of course that wouldn't work. This is completely different. Check it out.

12 INT – STAGE

DEFENSE ATTORNEY

Your honor, my client is innocent. The evidence clearly shows that the crime was committed by a right-handed person, and my client lost the use of his right arm ten years ago in an agricultural accident. I move for dismissal.

The camera shows the accused. He looks up, takes his left hand, lifts his right arm and lets it fall on the table. The judge looks at the accused, then at the Defense Attorney, then picks up a paper from the desk and stares at it.

JUDGE

Fair enough. Case dismissed. (He bangs the gavel.) Hey, whiskey, everyone?

They all break into a dance and start to form a conga line. The jury joins them. A guitar band appears, people put on big straw hats, and a celebration ensues.

13 INT – BOARD ROOM

Silence. Head Writer has his face in his hands. Writer 1, Writer 2 and Writer 3 stare at Writer 4. Writer 4 smiles.

Fade out.

Chapter 4 - Standup Comedy
Driving Around

———

AT THE BEGINNING OF the pandemic, during lockdown, one of the things I was able to do was drive around, but here's the deal: I don't like driving around.

For one thing, I have trouble with signs. They're doing construction on the Interstate near where I live, and there's a sign there I don't understand. Because I don't want to hit a highway worker, but if I do you'll give me $10,000? Fine!

There's a sign in the window of my gas station – "Attendant on duty cannot open safe." Don't rub it in! We don't need a sign for everything this guy can't do. "Attendant on duty can't go five minutes without looking at his phone." "Attendant on duty can't hold a job long enough to move out of his parents' basement." Come on! The guy already feels bad about working in a gas station.

A sign at the mall got me in trouble the other day. It said, "15 Minute Parking." I said, "How convenient!" So I parked there, then spent an hour looking for a store called "15 Minute." I never did find it.

Which is too bad, because occasionally, I'd like to have a 15 Minute store. Sometimes I want to watch a football game, but not the whole thing – just the fourth quarter. I'd like to have a 15 Minute store because I want to be famous – have some fame – but not for a long stretch of time.

When I gave up and went back to my car, there was a guy sitting there in his car, waiting to park and he said, "Hey, pal! Can't you read the sign?"

I said, "I know, right? I'm as upset as you are."

Then we were both confused.

My neighborhood has no sidewalks, and when you pull in there's a sign, but I have two questions: Who are the Caution children? Why are they walking in the roadway? Someone should have a word with the Caution family about their children.

There's a stop sign in the parking lot of a nearby car dealership. That's fine, but there's another sign under it that says, "Heavy Pedestrian Traffic." I think that's an insult to skinny pedestrians. What are you supposed to do when you see a skinny one? Speed up and try to hit one? Do you get extra points because they're kind of skittish?

I was driving on the highway the other day and caught a sign out of the corner of my eye. It said either "Big Sports Bar" or "Big Sports Bra." So I stopped and went in there. Imagine my disappointment! It was just a bunch of guys sitting around, drinking beer and watching TV!

There was a sign on a fast food chicken place that said, "Open Sundays." I thought, "That's it? Just Sundays? How do they make any money doing that?" Then I noticed they were working out of the back of a Chick-Fil-A, and I thought "Now that makes sense."

The other reason I don't like driving around is my car. It's starting to fall apart. The speedometer stopped working. But I took care of that – I bought a pitch pipe. And now I roll over those bumps on the side of the highway to see how fast I'm going.

You know about those bumps, right? The ones that help you stay between the lines? The drunk bumps? Kids call them "Twitter strips."

The faster I go, the higher the pitch on the bumps so I simply match the sound of the tires to the sound on the pitch pipe. But if I roll over the bumps and hear RRRRthumpthumpRRRR, I don't care how fast I'm going but I think someone owes me $10,000!

So I'm thinking about getting a new car, but I can't decide between a Nissan Maxima and a Nissan Altima, so I think I'll compromise and get a Nissan Maltima, but it only comes in vanilla, chocolate and strawberry... because it's a Maltima.

It's made for people who like to text and drive because it's made for malti-tasking... because it's a Maltima.

You can get the steering wheel on the left or on the right because it's malti-lateral... because it's a Maltima.

You can get the on board computer to talk to you in one of several languages because it's malti-lingual. You know why? I think you do.

My First Wife Sally

LET ME TELL YOU ABOUT my first wife, Sally. We met in college when she came over to a friend and me...

Let me pause for a moment and address the grammar aficionados, because that last sentence is grammatically correct. She came over to me... she came over to a friend and me. You wouldn't say "She came over to I," so why would you say, "She came over to a friend and I."

Unless... I happened to be dressed as the letter "I," in which case you would say "She came over to I." At which point she may have said, "How is I today?" And I might have replied, "I is fine. How is you?" which would only make sense if she were dressed as the letter "U." Then she could have said, "U is fine as well. Thank you for asking, I." And then we had to leave together because a roadside stand needed us to help spell FRUIT.

But I digress.

She came over to a friend and me and said, "Could you two guys help me carry my trunk up to the dorm room?" So you knew that right away she saw in me potential... as a concierge.

"Yes, ma'am, I'll see to that directly. Enjoy your stay."

After we got married, that changed. Right, guys? You get married and that changes. That simple request morphed into...

"DAVID! DAVID!!! THE LAUNDRY BASKET'S FULL!"

"I'll see to that directly... darling. Enjoy your stay.

Her friends called me "The Project." They'd get together and one of them would ask, "So, how's The Project?"

Sally would respond, "Coming along, coming along. I have him doing laundry…"

"Good for you!"

"… on command!"

"Whoa! You go, girl!"

… followed by high-fives.

One day she said to me, "You know, I've been thinking."

I said, "Uh-oh." I mean, not out loud. I'm not an idiot. Out loud I said,

"And what is that, darling?"

"You know, when you get out of the shower, you take a clean, dry towel, wipe clean water off a clean body, and hang up a clean, wet towel."

"Yeah?"

"Next day, it's the same thing. Take the same towel, a clean dry towel, clean water, clean body, and wind up with a clean wet towel."

"Yeah?"

"Theoretically, we should never have to launder towels."

"You know what? You're right!"

But just to be safe, at our house we launder towels twice a year, typically during the vernal and autumnal equinoxes. When you set your clocks, replace the batteries in the smoke alarm, and do a load of towels.

She was an excellent kisser... a great kisser... world-class. A dangerously good kisser to the point I think the Surgeon General should have gotten involved and posted a warning under her lips: "Warning! Kissing these lips may lead to grandchildren!" WHAT??? That is not what I signed up for!

My wife's from Louisville. Of course, if you're from Louisville, you don't say Louisville, you say Luhahvull. Like a bad ventriloquist:

Ventriloquist: Hey, everybody, meet my friend Petey!

Petey: Hello.

Ventriloquist: Hey, Petey, where are you from?

Petey: Luhahvull.

Ventriloquist: I hear that's a nice town. You like living in Louisville?

Petey: No, it's Luhahvull.

Ventriloquist: Ok... You like living in Louie-vull?

Petey: No, it's Luhahvull.

Ventriloquist: Ok... you like living in Luhah-ville?

Petey: NO! It's LUH.. AH... VULL. LUHAHVULL!

Ventriloquist: Ok, ok. So... Luhahvull.

Petey: Yeah.

Ventriloquist: Where they make that baseball bat, the Luhahvull Slugger?

Petey: Yeah.

Ventriloquist: Named after King Luhah the Sixteenth of France?

Petey: That's the guy.

Ventriloquist: The one who built Ver-sails?

Petey: I guess.

Ventriloquist: So... Luhahvull.

Petey: Yep.

Ventriloquist: Petey, are you sure it's not Louisville?

Petey: NO!!! IT'S LUHAHVULL!!! LUHAHVULL!!! AAARRRGGGHHH!!!"

(Petey attacks the ventriloquist, biting him on the nose. The ventriloquist screams and runs off stage.)

And she loved her lotion. I mean she REALLY loved her lotion. One morning, while attempting to shave in the shower, I noticed I was out of shaving cream. But there was a big bottle of lotion on the towel rack, so I used it instead. It worked fine. I said, "I'll pick up some shaving cream tonight," but I forgot.

So the next day, the same thing happened – I used the lotion and it worked fine. This went on for several days until I said, "You know, I wonder how long it would take me to use up all of this lotion." Let me tell you, it took months! It was a big bottle!

When I finally used up all the lotion in that bottle, I said, "You know, I wonder if she has more lotion." Let me tell you, she had more lotion. She had lotion with aloe in it. She had lotion with Vitamin D in it. She had lotion with vitamin E in it. She had lotion with bee pollen in it. Bee pollen! I didn't know whether to spread it on my face or on my toast!

She had lotion for her feet. She had exfoliating lotion for her legs. She had lotion for her hands. She had lotion for her face. She had lotion for her elbows. Her elbows. That's right, I said elbows.

Finally, came the grand and glorious day, and this was years later, I used up the last of my wife's lotion. I couldn't be more proud.

Maine

RECENTLY, I WAS IN the state of Maine. It's beautiful. While I was there, I went to an exhibition of the state horse.

I was talking to the guide and said, "Is there a leader of this group of horses? Leader of the pack, so to speak?"

He said, "Absolutely. It's that big stallion over there."

"So that's the main horse… of all of Maine's horses."

"Cute. That's cute."

"What do you call the hair on the back of its neck? It's beautiful."

"That's called a mane."

"So that's the mane… on the main horse… for the state of Maine."

"Clever. You're clever."

"I noticed he has knots tied in his hair, and some of the horses have their hair braided. Is it like that all year?"

"Most of the year, but for one month we take out the braids and the knots and let their hair relax."

"Really. What month is that?"

"Typically the month of May."

"So let me understand this. If I tied knots in horses' hair for a living, you would tell me that in the month of May I would not be permitted to tie knots in the hair of that stallion."

"Correct."

"But the rest of the year, I would be permitted to tie knots in the hair in the mane... of the main horse... for the state of Maine."

"You got it."

"So in May, I may not... knot... the main... Maine... mane... but if it's not May... I may knot... the main... Maine... mane."

"What?"

"In May I may not knot the main Maine mane but if it's not May I my knot the main Maine mane."

Then he said something I'll never forget. He turned away and yelled, "Security! Get this guy out of here. He's being an ass!"

I said, "An ass? I thought we were talking about horses!"

John Deer

ALTHOUGH WE LIVE ON a narrow lot in midtown, I recently bought a small John Deere tractor. I love my John Deere tractor. I have all the attachments – lawn mower, backhoe, snow plow.

Last fall I bagged a six-point buck, and recently I mounted its antlers on the front of my little tractor. I told my wife Wanda it wasn't a mule deer or a white-tailed deer; it was a John Deere deer.

Wanda was not amused, and said since I loved it so much, I should call it my dear John Deere. I told her she was mistaken, and it should be called my dear John Deere dear.

Wanda was not amused, and insisted I sell it. She said since I loved it so much, I should write it a Dear John letter. I told her she was mistaken, and it should be called a John Deere Dear John letter.

Wanda was not amused, and said I could write it a dear John Deere Dear John letter. I told her she was mistaken, and it should be called a dear John Deere deer Dear John letter.

Wanda was not amused , and said, "SELL IT! JUST SELL IT!"

So, if you know anyone that would like a small John Deere tractor, have them contact me.

Emoji Rap

I'VE STARTED USING the phrase "Kids these days." When did that start? Anyway, kids these days like their rap music, which I do not understand. Rap is music without melody. Have you ever heard a young man walking down the street, whistling his favorite rap song?

No you have not!

And kids these days like their emoji's, which I do not understand. Using emoji's is corresponding without words. Have you ever overheard two teenage girls, and one of them says, "This weekend, Jeremy said to me, 'Cupid, arrow, heart, sunset.' Isn't he just sugar cube cloud?"

No, you have not!

Recently my son said he was proud of me because I'd started to listen to rap music. I told him he was mistaken, and what I said was, "The last time I fell, I heard my hip pop."

I don't rap. But if I did, I'd probably be the oldest rapper in the entire room.

I don't rap. But if I were an old rapper during a time of COVID vaccinations, my rap name would be 2Shots.

I don't rap. But if I were an old rapper named 2Shots I'd rap about things kids love – emoji's.

I don't rap. But if I were an old rapper named 2Shots rapping about emoji's it might go a little something like this:

I love my baby. My baby's all that.

Smiley face, smiley face, winky face, cat.

My baby's so hot, she make me feel loopy.

Fire, fire, fire, poopy.

Got to show her I love her, got to show her I care.

Unicorn, unicorn, teddy bear.

Gonna pop the question 'cause I think we're ready.

Ring, ring, church, confetti.

I'm Old

I'M OLD. AS YOU KNOW, old age is the unfortunate side effect of not dying. And I have all the signs of old age. I occasionally get the day of the week from my pill box. I'll say, "Would you look at that? It's already W. Seems like just yesterday it was F. Where does the time go?"

I don't worry about the long term effects of anything. Just the other day I was reading an article about the long term effects of cell phone usage on the… I don't care!!! It's not my problem!!!

I hurt my elbow, but I'm old and didn't want to wait for Tommy John surgery, so I got Jimmy John surgery. It was freaky fast. Now my elbow works great, but it smells like a ham and cheese sandwich… with pickles and onions. I like it!

I've started ending conversations with my children with "I love you" because at this point, every conversation is potentially my last conversation. The other day I was on the phone with my daughter and at the end of the conversation I said, "I love you." She said, "I love you, too." Then just for fun I said, "I love you more." She said, "I wouldn't be surprised."

Old people are more vulnerable to street crime, so I signed up for what I thought was a short course in martial arts. It turns out there was a typo; it was a short course in *marital* arts. But it wasn't a complete waste of time because the two have a lot in common.

In martial arts, as a sign of respect you bow to the sensei and say "Taekwon." In *marital* arts, you bow to your spouse and say, "Yes, dear."

In martial arts, there's a defensive move – the down block. In *marital* arts, there's a defensive move – "No, that does not make your butt look big."

In martial arts, there's a crippling move – a side kick to the knee. In *marital* arts, there a crippling move – "I heard you the first time."

Old people need to stay active, so I joined a fitness club. Now I do what we in the fitness community call "progressions." I start with a little cardio on the elliptical machine, and from there I progress to going home. So right now, it's just a two-step progression. But since I started working out, I have fewer back issues... of National Geographic! See what I did there? Back issues? Ha!

I've started going to venues that cater to my demographic. There's a new one in town. It's not a biker bar or a country music bar; it's a fiber bar. It's well-lit. All the tables are wheel chair accessible. There's always a little Barry Manilow playing in the background.

They have a limited à la carte menu, but they do have tapioca, broth, pudding... anything that can be eaten with or without teeth.

At the bar they have herbal tea, vitamin water... but their signature drink is Jell-O shots made with lime Jell-O and prune juice. They call it "The Shooter."

I've started using the phrase "kids these days." I'm not even sure when that started.

Kids these days have some strange weddings. I was at a wedding recently where two CrossFit instructors got married. The bride, the bridesmaids, the groom and the groomsmen all wore matching tank tops, shorts, gym socks and Reeboks. The bride came down the aisle doing lunges. On the altar the bride and the groom were on facing treadmills.

At the end of the ceremony the minister turned to the groom and said, "You may kiss the bride." He lay down on a bench getting ready to do a bench press. The bride stood above him getting ready to do a push up. They held hands, and as he flexed his arms for the bench press, she lowered herself for the pushup, and their lips met for their first wedded kiss. It was lovely. But they weren't done because they had to do ten reps.

At the reception the bride, instead of throwing a bouquet, threw a kettle weight. The bridesmaids just scattered.

And kids these days are always showing us their underwear, which I do not understand. If you see a young man walking down the street in the summer, you'll see his underpants pooching out. And young women are always showing us their bra straps. I don't get it, because no one wants to see an old man's underwear.

Wait... you do? You want to look old and young at the same time?

Boom!

About the Author

David G Scott is a retired college professor, a grandfather, an Army veteran and a proud member of the Subway Rewards Program.

www.ingramcontent.com/pod-product-compliance
Lightning Source LLC
Chambersburg PA
CBHW051214160726
47994CB00002B/597